Destination Known

A Story of Replenished Faith and Renewed Joy

EMILY WOLF

WESTBOW
PRESS®
A DIVISION OF THOMAS NELSON
& ZONDERVAN

Scripture quotations marked ESV taken from The Holy Bible, English Standard Version® (ESV®) Copyright © 2001 by Crossway, a publishing ministry of Good News Publishers. All rights reserved.

Scripture quotations marked KJV are taken from the King James Version of the Bible.

Scripture quotations marked NCV are taken from the New Century Version® Copyright © 2005 by Thomas Nelson. Used by permission. All rights reserved.

Scripture quotations marked NIV are taken from The Holy Bible, New International Version®, NIV® Copyright © 1973, 1978, 1984, 2011 by Biblica, Inc.® Used by permission. All rights reserved worldwide.

Scripture quotations marked NKJV are taken from the New King James Version® Copyright © 1982 by Thomas Nelson. Used by permission. All rights reserved.

WestBow Press books may be ordered through booksellers or by contacting:

WestBow Press
A Division of Thomas Nelson & Zondervan
1663 Liberty Drive
Bloomington, IN 47403
www.westbowpress.com
1 (866) 928-1240

Because of the dynamic nature of the Internet, any web addresses or links contained in this book may have changed since publication and may no longer be valid. The views expressed in this work are solely those of the author and do not necessarily reflect the views of the publisher, and the publisher hereby disclaims any responsibility for them.

Any people depicted in stock imagery provided by Getty Images are models, and such images are being used for illustrative purposes only.
Certain stock imagery © Getty Images.

ISBN: 978-1-9736-5312-7 (sc)
ISBN: 978-1-9736-5311-0 (e)

Print information available on the last page.

WestBow Press rev. date: 2/13/2019

Dedication

I DEDICATE THIS BOOK TO EVERYONE; TO ALL WHO ARE hopeless, for each person finding it hard to put on foot in front of the other day by day, for everyone searching for hope, peace, and joy. I pray our story inspires you to hold onto the hope of our future in heaven and to open your eyes to all the beauty and blessings of this earth along the way. Our destination is known; we have heaven ahead of us.

I dedicate this book to my husband and my son. Seth is the reason for this book. His heart is so full of Christ, and I am so thankful Seth has shown me God's love and changed my life. Seth will never know how much he is my hero.

My husband, whose motto is "Keep it simple," has shown me not to sweat the small stuff. He taught me what really matters in life. He is a simple man who works hard and loves harder. He is my treasured gift from God, and I pray he knows how much I appreciate the beauty, joy, and love he has given to my life.

He and Seth have brought me closer to God. The trials we have faced together have been stepping stones for a complete transformation of our faith. Our faith continues to grow and I hope our story inspires you.

I hope this book helps you find peace in the tough times, joy through sorrow, and hope even when all hope seems lost for our ultimate destination—heaven. "He restores my soul" (Psalm 23:3 NKJV).

Emily Wolf with her husband, Matt, and son, Seth

1 Longing for Heaven

HOW OFTEN DOES YOU FUTURE CROSS YOUR MIND? I'M SURE you think about your job, your family, or even that vacation you have planned. But how often do you think about your ultimate future we will all face? We will all pass away from this earth, and that is the most important fact about life. Sounds odd that the sole point of living is dying, but it's the truth. This life we know and live isn't our final destination.

This earth isn't our home; heaven is. Heaven is our future. Heaven is our hope. We should all live with excitement that we are heaven-bound, that no matter the pain we face on earth, we can look forward to an eternity of perfect peace with God. We will one day get to wrap our arms around our heavenly Father and live with Him forever. What a glorious thought that is much more than just a thought! It is more than a dream. It is the promise of God to us, the ultimate gift at the end of our journeys on earth.

God gives us life-changing love. "For God so loved the world that he gave his one and only Son, that whosoever believes in Him shall not perish but have everlasting life" (John 3:16 NIV) is a popular scripture, a beautiful and amazing promise from the lips of God Himself. If you really meditate on what this means, it will change you, shape your perspective, and nourish your soul.

We should all think more about our eternal life rather than our earthly life. Our focus should be on our greatest future endeavor—heaven. The promise of heaven should be a constant and daily source of joy, peace, and hope.

I did not come to these epiphanies on my own; they did not come to me in prayer. God sent this lesson to me through my son. I had never thought much of heaven. It surely wasn't something that crossed my mind each day until my son changed that.

Seth was seven as I started to write this book. He was longed for and prayed for and is the greatest blessing in my husband's and my lives. Our Seth is loving, kind, beautiful, and sweet. Yet life with our sweet Seth has been challenging. I call Seth Super Seth. He struggles but inspires me daily. He hears God clearly. He has an unshakeable bond with Jesus that most of us yearn for. For Seth, it comes naturally just like breathing. It is his existence.

As a toddler, Seth spoke of Jesus. Each time he did, he would smile and find special peace. Peace is hard for Seth to find. He was diagnosed with autism two months before his second birthday. His first two years were full of struggles with feeding, endless crying, anxiety, and pain. His diagnosis wasn't a shock; it was more of a relief that Seth could receive the help he needed.

Years of therapy and heartache led to little progression and instead regression. After six years of searching for answers to why Seth was dealing with chronic fatigue, muscle weakness, and pain, in 2018, God blessed us with an answer. He has a gene abnormality that commonly caused congenital muscular myopathy.

I write of Seth's struggles and diagnosis because his journey is important; his hardships are his stepping stones to God. He seeks the Lord for encouragement when he is feeling low and for laughter when he's upset. He seeks the Lord for the promise of peace from the pain and sorrow he faces. Seth seeks Jesus, feels Him, knows Him, and adores Him. Most of all, Seth yearns for heaven so he can be with Him.

Seth's special bond with Jesus became clear when he was a

toddler. He would see Jesus crosses as he called them everywhere—telephone poles, sticks, lines in the sky—he saw them all around. He would also draw them every chance he got. If he had paper and a marker, you could bet he would draw cross. He would draw them with his little fingers in the dirt outside. It was incredible to watch. As Seth became more verbal, we began to witness how astounding his relationship with the Lord really was and is.

I had always planned to raise Seth in the church. I loved our church family, and I looked forward to Seth growing up in this family as well. Those plans changed, and as with many other happenings in Seth's life's and ours, I learned to never make plans. God is the only one who is all knowing. Seth's anxiety and his sensory and transition issues made going to church worship an impossible struggle. Despite our best efforts to modify church to make it work, we decided to have church worship and Bible study at home. My heart was hurt, but that taught me that God was in control and that plans changed.

I had always wanted our family to grow up knowing Christ, and God took care of that. He knows the desires of our hearts and cares for us, His children. He has drawn so near to my sweet Seth, closer than I could have ever foreseen or imagined.

Seth began to say incredible things. As he would sit outside watching the wind blow through the trees, he would say, "Jesus is making the trees dance." Seth finds calm in nature because he finds God there. He stares deeply into the clouds, smiles, and says, "Jesus just told me He loves me."

Through the closeness and love Seth and the Lord share with each other, my life has been transformed. I have an entirely different view on life in the best way. I stand in awe at what God will do for us. I stand amazed by His promises, and I bow in thanksgiving. I know that this story of Seth's longing for heaven will transform your life and heart as well.

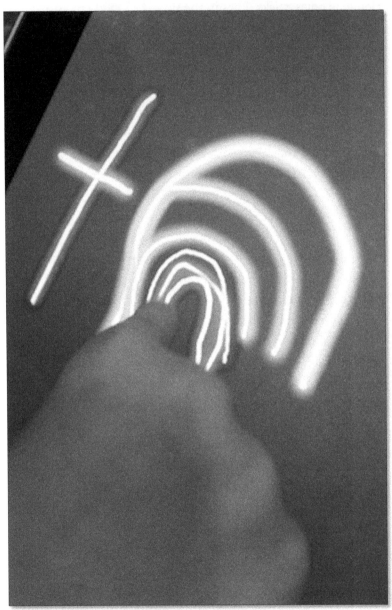

Seth drawing crosses on his tablet

Seth holding a tiny cross he made with sticks

A heart-shaped leaf Seth found

Seth creating more crosses with sticks

A heart shape made by a caterpillar in a leaf

2 Dwell

S ETH HAS SHOWN ME TIME AND AGAIN THAT FOCUSING ON
Jesus is the only way to live. "Looking unto Jesus, the author
and finisher of our faith" (Hebrews 12:2 KJV). Jesus is a constant
on His mind. He speaks of him throughout the day, and he strives
to make Him proud. At night, he sweetly prays, "I wanna to be
sweet like you, Jesus." He inherently knows Jesus is pure love. He
speaks so profoundly yet with such childlike innocence.

Seth told me at a very young age, "You know Jesus is never mad
or grumpy?" Seth knows the truth because it's written in his precious
soul. "Truly I say to you, unless you turn and become like children,
you will never enter the kingdom of Heaven" (Matthew 18:3 ESV).

We should all have open hearts, deep faith, and total
dependence on God just as children have with their parents. We
should live to make Him happy just as children yearn to please
their parents. Seth has always had a deep desire to make Jesus
proud solely because he loves Him so deeply that he wants to please
Him. He tells me often when he does something nice, "Jesus is so
proud that He's doing a happy dance right now."

That thought makes me smile! Why wouldn't Jesus rejoice
when we follow His ways? He is our number-one cheerleader, so
of course He gets excited when we follow Him. God loves us so
deeply and longs for us to love and trust Him. Just as we trusted
our parents growing up and knew they would meet our basic needs,

we should even more trust in God knowing without a doubt that we are in His loving hands. We should come to the Lord with full trust and unending faith. We should admiring Him and all He is. We should long to be like Him in every way. He is the great I Am. He is all we will ever need. He is our reason for being. He is our future in heaven.

"Finally brothers, whatever is true, whatever is honorable, whatever is just, whatever is pure, whatever is commendable, if there is any excellence, if there is anything worthy of praise, think on these things" (Philippians 4:8 ESV). It's clear what God wants our minds to dwell on—Him and all things good. We should rebuke negative and discontented thoughts. We should try our best to remove the weary words in our minds that are dragging us down. God will replace them with truth and show us all that is beautiful in our lives.

When it seems peace is fleeing your life, dwell on Jesus. Dwell on the truth in His holy Word. Dwell on His excellence, which surrounds us. Dwell on His beauty, His grace. Dwell on heaven. "For as a man thinks in his heart, so is he" (Proverbs 23:7 KJV). When we turn our minds from our stresses and to the Lord, our lives will change. God is working on us daily. It is a daily choice to fill our minds with the right thoughts. Only God can help us recognize and defeat the negative. Our thoughts determine our actions, and our actions determine our life. Choose to dwell on Christ. "Be careful what you think, because your thoughts run your life" (Proverbs 4:23 NCV).

Seth chooses to focus on Jesus rather than his struggles. He tells me often that he won't have these struggles in heaven. He tells me of the awesome toys and the cozy blankets in heaven, all the beautiful, childlike things he fills his mind with. I know this comes from God Himself. He speaks to Seth and shows him special things.

Seth has taught me how looking toward Jesus each day lifts our outlook on life. One of my favorite stories of Seth's special bond with Jesus is when Seth saw Jesus right in front of him. We had to travel three hours for an appointment with a specialist, and Seth struggled on long car rides. He felt frustrated; it was hard on him. A fourth of the way into this drive, Seth was already melting down and screaming, and all we could do was keep driving. It is never good when you cannot offer your child help or comfort.

I was trying to stay calm and positive for him, but the situation was wearing on me. I was on the verge of my own mommy meltdown. Then suddenly Seth stopped screaming, looked directly in front of him, and started laughing! He giggled with joy. My husband and I were totally baffled but so relieved he was not only calm but also laughing.

After a few minutes of giggles, Seth calmly looked out the window with a smile across his little face; he seemed so relaxed and content. I asked him what was so funny but got no response. Then several minutes later, Seth said, "Mommy, I laughed so hard because Jesus was being funny to me." I was stunned, but I immediately thanked the Lord. Then I just smiled and giggled a bit to myself. I felt so relaxed and content as well.

Jesus is always with us and ready to help anyway He can, but how often do we miss His holy presence because we're focused on other things and end up missing His almighty outreached hand? He's there just waiting to give us joy, just waiting to give us laughter and peace when life is tough.

I learned that day that as much as I wanted Seth to have joy in life, God wanted that even more for Seth. We are all God's children, and He will always comfort us. We need to focus on Him and open our eyes—He's right in front of us.

Seth lives this verse: "Set your minds on things above, not on earthly things." He has taught me how important this is. It is the only way to live and walk through this life. Seth's mind is set on heaven. He lights up with joy when he talks about heaven. He deals with a lot in his little life. His autism makes life tough. With it, autism brings sensory issues, motor delays, learning delays, and communication issues as well. He can't handle noises or crowds, and he has debilitating anxiety. His muscular myopathy presents with a whole host of other issues as well; muscle pain, weakness, chronic fatigue, scoliosis, and basic body functioning issues make for hard days. He spends much of his days resting to conserve his energy. Yet when Seth speaks of heaven, I realize he has the one thing most everyone else is missing—hope. The hope of heaven. Thinking and dwelling on the promise of heaven gives Seth comfort.

When he is unable to walk because his legs are tired and hurting, he tells me, "Do you know my legs will never hurt in heaven? Nothing ever hurts in heaven." When he gets worn out from any activity, his weary little mouth speaks, "I'll never get tired out in heaven. I can play and never feel tired. Isn't that the best? I can't wait!"

I used to feel sad that Seth would much prefer to be in heaven than here on earth until I realized that is exactly the way we should all live! This earth is not our home, and life can be tough, but heaven is our hope, our home. We should all have such an overwhelming and deep love for God that we want to be with Him more than anyone else.

Seth knows heaven will bring him total peace. When he struggles through a meltdown, he calls them his grumpies. He pleads with me to make it better; he tells me the grumpies are too strong. These meltdowns can last hours and be filled with violence and despair, but that's not my sweet boy at all, just his earthly struggles.

I stopped in my tracks when he told me, "There are no

grumpies in heaven. No one is ever sad, mad, or grumpy." I love thinking about that thought. I am thankful Seth reminds me to dwell on this truth: "And God shall wipe away all tears from their eyes, and there shall be no more death, neither sorrow, nor crying, neither shall there be any more pain: for the former things are passed away" (Revelation 21:4 KJV). How much peace that truth brings. How much peace it gives Seth. He knows so much yet has not been exposed to these Bible truths in school or church. He gets them straight from God Himself.

I pray we all find peace dwelling on the promise of heaven. How amazing it is to know that no matter what, there will be an end to all the pain we face in our lives. We should focus on that. We should focus on hope in a hopeless world. The hope of heaven. The joy of heaven. The promise of an eternity with God.

Seth attends a small homeschool in our town. He would only go two hours a day a couple days a week due to his fatigue. He would always struggle about going, but he ended up always enjoying his time there. He was even able to play on the playground with his friends. He always told me that was his favorite part of his day.

For a year, Seth was unable to attend that school, so I started homeschooling him myself. He told me that school was too much for him because he would get too tired. I already knew that was the reason, but Seth being able to verbalize that made me feel we were making the right decision for him.

But my mommy heart ached so deeply. I was grateful Seth expressed these things to me, but hearing it broke my heart. I held him close and said, "I know you get tired, but we are seeing more doctors, and hopefully, they can help you and you could get back to class. You'd be back in action, buddy! Would that be awesome?"

Seth just sat quietly with his thoughts and said, "My body will never get tired in heaven, and I'll be able to run super-fast! Jesus will run with me, and we'll even have races!" He spoke with such excitement and hope just like that. The promise of heaven overwhelmed Seth's precious soul, and he was encouraged. He was smiling.

Seth has hope beyond this world. We all have this hope offered to us; we just have to realize it, dwell on it, and accept it. We have to treasure it, hold it dear, and let it be a constant reminder in our hearts. No matter what, heaven awaits us. No matter what, we will be wrapped in Jesus's perfect arms in perfect peace with Him forever.

3 Quick Return

ONE EVENING WHEN WE WERE WATCHING THE SUNSET, SETH told me the most incredible thing. He said he wasn't sad to leave heaven. My mind raced. *What? Huh? How?* Seth said, "I wasn't sad to leave heaven. I miss heaven. But Jesus told me when I came to live with you and daddy that I shouldn't worry because I would be back really fast, fast-fast! But I can't wait to go back and give Jesus a big hug!" So matter of factly he spoke. He has been in heaven. He recalls things about it, and he longs to return there. Yet amazingly, his young soul knows life is very short. "What is your life? You are a mist that appears for a little while and then vanishes" (James 4:14 NIV). It is true in God's own words—the life we have on earth is fleeting, temporary; it goes by very quickly or as Seth would say, "fast-fast."

Seth knows without a doubt he will be back with Jesus soon. He showed me that just the other night in our living room. "Mommy, watch this. This is what I'm gonna do when I get back to heaven." Then he ran around the living room happily shouting, "Jesus!" and leaped on the couch and hugged a pillow with all his might. He said he would hug Jesus tightly. The joy in his eyes—unmatchable. His hope for heaven—awe inspiring. Wow. What if we all thought of how we will react upon returning home? Seth thinks every day of his reunion with Jesus. He longs for it. He plans for it. He gets out of this world excited for it! We should all have such excitement for the end of our time on earth.

Seth explained to me that he could do whatever he wanted in heaven. He said the first thing he would do when He got to heaven was to fly. Seth stretched out his arms and said, "Just like this I'll be able to fly. Jesus told me!"

He looks forward to his future in heaven so much; he has an utter zeal for his welcome back home. "But our citizenship is in heaven, and we eagerly await a Savior there, the Lord Jesus Christ" (Philippians 3:20 NIV).

We are of heaven, not of earth. Heaven is our perfect home with our perfect Father. Home sweet home—such a sweet, comforting phrase. So much comfort and peace lies in our earthly homes, but how much more lies in our heavenly home?

My husband lost a dear friend and coworker this year. We often seek Seth's wisdom, and it always brings us comfort. One evening, my husband asked Seth, "You think my friend is having fun in heaven?" Seth's response was awe inspiring and beyond profound: "He is having so much fun in heaven he doesn't even miss anything. Because when you're in heaven, it's so awesome that you never miss the whole world. You never want to leave heaven, you never miss anything, you are just so happy and having so much fun." If we could always remember this truth.

If we always focused on the incredible gift of our heavenly home, our lives would be full of peace, comfort, and hope. How sweet our home will be! "Show me O Lord my life's end and the number of my days. Let me know how fleeting my life is" (Psalm 39:4 NIV). Our time on earth is indeed fleeting. Realizing how brief our time on earth is has given me indescribable peace and undeniable hope. I can have such a painful day and can see such sorrow in this world, yet I hear God constantly saying to me, "This is temporary."

When I get overwhelmed, God sends Seth to give me the simplest reminders that everything will be okay one day. One day, all the despair will make sense. Seth randomly comes to me with thoughts of heaven. "Mommy, Jesus told me they have the coziest blankets ever in heaven." I remember to focus on heaven, focus on going home. Something as simple and childlike as soft blankets sends my mind into an extraordinary dream world of how incredible heaven will be. Our minds cannot fathom the peace or comprehend the beauty of heaven.

Seth often speaks of the beautiful things in heaven. Rainbow trees and birds with butterfly wings. Simply amazing to dream of heaven. Makes my soul smile. Life on earth is solely about heaven. Heaven is near because my life is fleeting. Heaven is beyond amazing. What joy comes with these realizations. "Teach us to number our days, that we may gain a heart of wisdom" (Psalm 90:12 NIV).

Wisdom is knowledge and good judgement. Knowing from God's Word that our time on earth is brief, that our days are numbered, helps us go forward each day with hope and joy because we know one day, joy is all there will ever be. Pain and sadness are momentary while joy and peace are eternal.

So think about, plan, and look forward with excitement to our quick return home! "I consider that our present sufferings are not worth comparing with the glory that will be revealed in us" (Romans 8:18 NIV).

4 Good Grief

"OH GOOD GRIEF!"—A PHRASE MADE FAMOUS BY THE ONE and only Charlie Brown. But when praying about what to write in this book, waiting for God to lead me to the words He needed me to write, these came to mind: "Good grief." That statement is an oxymoron; grief is the opposite of good. Yet from God's view, grief can be for good. "And we know that in all things God works for the good of those who love Him, who have been called according to His purpose" (Romans 8:28 NIV).

This can be hard to grasp especially when we are facing inconsolable grief. Life on earth can bring tragedy, loss, and sadness that leave an empty place in our souls. We can find it hard to put one foot in front of the other to get through the day. Grief on earth can seem impossible to live with. We can feel hopeless. Yet God is a God of truth. He says He will work all for our good, and He will. One day, it will all make sense. One day, even if that day isn't until heaven, we will know the meaning of our grief.

Jesus stated in the Beatitudes,

> Blessed are the poor in spirit, for theirs is the kingdom of heaven. Blessed are those who mourn, for they will be comforted. Blessed are the meek, for they will inherit the earth. Blessed are those who hunger and thirst for righteousness, for they

will be filled. Blessed are the merciful, for they will be shown mercy. Blessed are the pure in heart, for they will see God. Blessed are the peacemakers, for they will be called children of God. Blessed are those who are persecuted because of righteousness, for theirs is the kingdom of Heaven. (Matthew 5:3–10 NIV)

We will be comforted in heaven and see God. No matter what, God is before us. It will all be okay. In the meantime, we are called to focus and rely on God to carry us through our grief on earth. Trust His plan, follow His path. "Trust in the Lord with all your heart and lean not on your own understanding" (Proverbs 3:5 NIV).

Last year when I was praying about how overwhelming the thought of Seth's future was, I felt lost, sad, angry, confused, and overwhelmed. But God spoke clearly to me: "Take this one day at a time, I will give you each day your daily bread."

Jesus said,

This then is how you should pray, our Father in Heaven, Holy is your name, Your kingdom come, your will be done on earth as it is in Heaven. GIVE US THIS DAY OUR DAILY BREAD. Forgive us our debts, as we also have forgiven our debtors. Lead us not into temptation but deliver us from the evil one. (Matthew 6:9–13 NIV; emphasis mine)

Day by day, step by step, God will carry us. We will have what we need for each day; we must receive this gift. His almighty strength and power are ours for the taking. "I can do all things through Christ who strengthens me" (Philippians 4:13 NKJV).

"He gives strength to the weary and increases the power of the weak" (Isaiah 40:29 NIV). I praise God and am so grateful for these promises. I wouldn't be here without His strength.

He has carried me through my darkest days and has reminded me that alone, I am weak but with Him, I am strong. I am also reminded that the Lord fully understands our earthly weakness and struggles. Jesus lived and walked this same earth fully human. He was betrayed, tempted, tortured, and murdered. Jesus himself had horrific suffering and pain on this earth. His life wasn't easy, and ours will not be either. God carried Him through it all; He turned the worst into the best—our salvation.

Jesus knew without a doubt that God would care for Him and that He had a great plan. The Lord knows firsthand how we feel; that is why the magnificent strength of our Father is gifted to us. Without Him, we will fail, but with Him, we will prevail and reach our ultimate destination, heaven. "Blessed is the man who remains steadfast under trial, for when he has stood the test he will receive the crown of life, which God has promised to those who love Him" (James 1:12 ESV).

Grief is not good, but God is. He will erase all the sadness, pain, and grief soon. Until then, we walk with faith and a smile knowing we have the strength of the almighty. We know that He will work all for good and that we have all the greatness of heaven ahead of us.

5 The Small Things

SETH HAS ALWAYS HAD AN INCREDIBLE GIFT FOR NOTICING details. This is likely why he cannot tolerate new places, crowds, large rooms, and loud environments. He is unable to filter out the details or unnecessary information as most of us can. I've come to realize this is a gift. Seth has taught me how to notice the beauty of details and the small things in life.

When he was a baby, Seth would cry for hours, but sometimes, he would be soothed by watching a fire crackle in the fireplace. Sitting out in the breeze would also help him find a calm place. Seth found escape even just watching his little fish swim around in their tank. To this day, Seth still finds his peace in nature. He notices anything including rocks and shadows that are shaped like hearts. He notices lines in the sidewalk that look like crosses. Details we all walk right over.

He stands in the breeze outside with his arms outstretched and his eyes closed just breathing in the peace of the wind. He can watch rain fall on the pavement for the longest time. He says when they hit the concrete, it looks like fireworks. You know, if you take the time to notice, it looks exactly like that! It is beautiful. We are all so rushed, stressed, and focused on the wrong things that we miss out on the small but spectacular details of life, the details that make an ordinary day simply amazing.

God made the most beautiful world for us to enjoy; it's filled with amazing sunsets, rainbows, scenery, and creatures. "In the beginning God created the Heaven and the earth" (Genesis 1:1 NIV). "God saw all that He had made and it was very good" (Genesis 1:31 NIV). God gave us earth—a beautiful but temporary home. Nature that surrounds us each day is His almighty beauty right before our eyes. I used to gripe and complain that I didn't get to go on vacations to see beauty and scenery; I felt being constantly stuck at home was so unfair. I was so discontent and angry that I was missing out.

Now, I'd still love a vacation, but it would be for different reasons. My mind-set was totally wrong. I was missing out on the incredible beauty right in front of my eyes each day. God and Seth changed my heart completely. When you focus on what you have instead of what you are missing, your life changes. I missed out on blessings because I was discontent with where God had me, but I opened my eyes. Now, I can sit in my backyard and get the essence of a vacation just by looking at the sky, by enjoying butterflies, or by watching the sky's colors changing in the evening.

Right here, right now, my life is beautiful. I can escape into the beauty God has placed before me. I am so grateful. "Praise Him, sun and moon; praise Him, all you shining stars. Praise Him, you highest Heavens, and you waters above the skies. Let them praise the name of the Lord, For at His commanded they were created" (Psalm 148:3–5 NIV).

I don't trudge through each day looking for more; I fully enjoy and engage with all I am given. Deep breaths of fresh air are so rejuvenating as are quick escapes to peaceful places I had overlooked. Blowing bubbles with Seth, I am mesmerized at swirls of colors within each bubble. Wildflowers are so unique, detailed, and gorgeous.

I constantly enjoy and praise God for the details I used to walk right past. The small things, the details, are the glue that holds the masterpiece of this world together. Take time to lose yourself in the small things each day and your soul will be renewed.

Seth has taught me to focus of the beauty of this world and the beauty beyond this world. Seth has amazing stories of what heaven is like; he recalls being with Jesus, and he dreams of how amazing heaven will be as well. He says, "There is always shining light in heaven, not the sun because heaven is way farther than outer space. In heaven, it's never ever dark." "And there shall be no night there and they need no candle, neither light of the sun; for the Lord God giveth them light: and they shall reign forever and ever" (Revelation 22:5 KJV).

I can only imagine the small things in heaven. I know that there are no small things, that heaven will be mighty and remarkable. Such comforting and inspiring thoughts to ponder. We can only begin to imagine the glory and gorgeousness of our eternal home. The grand wonder of it all should be the foundation of our daily life. We should not let the small things pass us by. We should go out, watch the trees, feel the breeze, and soak up the sun knowing that each beautiful detail is of God and He has even more in store for us. "The Heavens declare the glory of God; the skies proclaim the work of His hands" (Psalm 19:1 NIV). God's work is astounding; it will turn ordinary details into works of art. At times, the Lord reveals Himself in nature. Seth has seen this, and it is a day I will never forget.

While watching the sunset one evening in August 2014, Seth looked up, pointed to the sky, and said, "Jesus is right there." I always have my phone handy capture our sunsets and nature pictures, so I snapped a picture to document the moment Seth saw Jesus!

Two minutes later, Seth said, "He's gone now. He was right there on that cloud, but he left." Seth was entranced and smiling from the inside out of his soul and almost singing from within for joy. He had seen Jesus! Seth said, "I can't believe I saw Him! This is the best day ever!" We rejoiced in the moment.

I stand in awe at how apparent the Lord is to Seth. Jesus is always with us, and Seth is always in tune with Jesus, always thinking of Him and sending Him love, hugs, and songs. He talks to Him in his heart, and that day, he saw Him, the Lord of all creation right there and looking down.

That evening when praying, Seth said, "Thank you, Jesus, for showing me where you were on that cloud today." I was silent. Seth knew how unbelievably special that was. He often tells me, "I know Jesus is in my heart. I can feel Him, but I just can't see Him." Well, that summer day, Seth got a miraculous glimpse of his Father, his best friend, his everything, and he was thankful. So was I.

Seth's heart fully belongs to the Lord. I learn firsthand each day that the only way to live is longing for Jesus, loving Him more than anything, and relishing the undeniable beauty of this earth. We should seek His face. "But if from there you seek the Lord your God, you will find Him with all your heart and with all your soul" (Deuteronomy 4:29 NIV).

Seth basking in the breeze

The sunlight made a beautiful cross

Seth pointing at the sky when he saw Jesus on the cloud

6 Hand in Hand

SETH STRUGGLES DAILY WITH ANXIETY. HE IS ANXIOUS, fearful, and unable to be in a room alone. Someone needs to be in his sight. He has so much fear. This has been lifelong for Seth, and we cope with it the best we can.

When Seth needs a toy from his room, he asks someone to go along. We help however we are able. We sleep by his side. Rest for Seth is a top priority. To avoid Seth waking in a panic attack during the night, I sleep with him. Of course I often need to sneak out of the room while he is asleep; I pray he doesn't wake in a panic and is up for the rest of the night.

Last December, the Lord showed Himself to us in a way He never had before. It was a horrible morning filled with anxiety and violent meltdowns. I finally got Seth to calm down. Exhausted, he fell asleep for a nap. I was feeling so defeated, tired, and overwhelmed with the difficult days we faced. My heart was hurting for Seth and his struggles. I had to leave his bedside to walk Seth's new puppy. I always take a monitor with me so I can hear any signs of Seth waking up. I heard on my monitor, "Mommy." I went as fast as I could and braced myself for the panic attack I was sure he would have. I lay next to him and put my hand on his back. He wasn't shaking, scared, or crying. I told him I had heard him call my name, and I asked if he had been looking for me. His answer knocked the breath from my lungs and pushed me to my knees. "I wasn't scared because Jesus was holding my hand."

My world stopped. I was stunned with amazement and joy. I thanked the Lord for being so present to my baby while I was gone and for revealing to me that He was always holding our hands. Always. Incredible! "Do not fear, for I am with you. Do not be dismayed for I am your God. I will strengthen you and help you. I will uphold you with my righteous right hand" (Isaiah 41:10 NIV).

I gathered my thoughts after my beautiful shock and asked Seth if he had seen Jesus. His response once again left me breathless. "I couldn't see Him, but I could feel Him holding my hand. Even though Jesus lives in my heart, He can still hold my hand because Jesus can do anything." Perfect, profound words from a six-year-old's heart. Seth struggles to express himself in the most basic ways, yet when he speaks of Jesus and heaven, he never pauses. So precise. His words flow so easily from his mind and his heart.

That day, Jesus showed me in the most up-front way that He was with us. Every second of every day, our almighty Father is by our side. "For I am the Lord your God who takes hold of your right hand and says to you, Do not fear, I will help you" (Isaiah 41:13 NIV).

Seth did not feel afraid. He was peaceful holding the hand of God. That day changed my life and continues to shape my heart. I don't have the fear and anxiety I once had. How could I fear knowing that God is walking by my side and is next to all my loved ones? He has us all in His hands. He has everything under His control. "I will instruct you and teach you in the way you should go; I will counsel you with my loving eye on you" (Psalm 32:8 NIV).

The love of my life, my husband, is a pilot. Aviation is his passion. I've always been plagued with extreme worry when he flies especially in the dark or in bad weather. My fear and worry have been relieved so much knowing God is alongside him. I picture God's hand carrying his plane to and from his destination. No matter what comes—good days, bad days, days filled with joy and laughter—I thank God, who is holding our hands as we walk through our earthly journey. There is nothing we cannot conquer with God by our side. One day, He will hold our hands for eternity. "The Lord is my light and my salvation. Whom shall I fear? The Lord is the stronghold of my life, of whom shall I be afraid?" (Psalm 27:1 NIV).

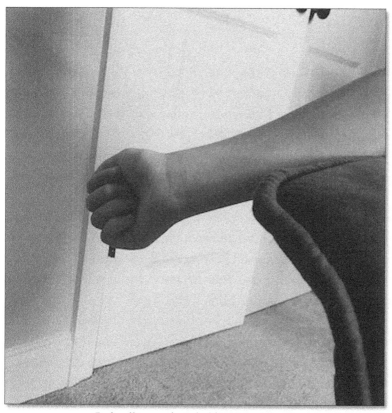

Seth telling me he is holding Jesus's hand

7 *Hakuna Matata*

"**H**AKUNA MATATA, WHAT A WONDERFUL PHRASE, HAKUNA matata it means no worries for the rest of your days." The Disney Movie *The Lion King* introduced us to this phrase. Seth does not watch Disney movies because they cause him anxiety, but I often use this phrase with him when he is stressed or worried. I sing the song aloud, and it makes Seth laugh. But honestly, they are words to live by.

Jesus told us the same thing: "Do not be anxious about anything, but in everything by prayer and petition, with thanksgiving, present your requests to God. And the peace of God, which transcends all understanding will guard your hearts and your minds in Christ Jesus" (Philippians 4:6–7 NIV).

As much as Seth is burdened by anxiety through no fault of his own, he still grasps that the Lord is in control. He often says, "I'll ask Jesus to tell me so I don't forget." Seth says that when he wants to remember to tell someone something or to do something. He asks Jesus to remind him knowing Jesus will not forget. Seth doesn't waste time trying to remember things; he just depends on Jesus. It is pretty amazing, and watching Seth wholeheartedly present simple things like that to the Lord has changed how I live.

We should all relax and not stress about every little thing. We should depend fully on God for the big and small things alike. "Ask and it will be given to you, seek and you will find; knock and the door will be opened to you" (Matthew 7:7 NIV). Straight to the point. How often we stress and get overwhelmed trying to do it all on our own; we forget to ask for help. Jesus will deliver even in the smallest ways.

Seth asks for help even with the simplest things every day. He will tell me, "I asked Jesus, and He helped me be brave." I am so blessed to have a special little boy reminding me of the way to live each day. We all have God doing the same thing, but we don't listen. We miss it. We keep going the wrong way, and it gets harder and harder to hear His voice. Seth is embedded in Christ as we all are; he is always speaking to Him, listening to Him, and laughing with Him.

The minute we decide to walk with God each second, anxiety leaves our lives. It is hard to be anxious when we focus on God and on heaven and ask Him to help us with anything and everything. God even tells us not to worry about anything, even the basic necessities.

> Do not be anxious about your life, what you will eat, nor about your body, what you will put on. For you life is more than food, and the body more than clothing. Consider the ravens; they neither sow nor reap, they have neither storehouse nor barn, and yet God feeds them. Of how much more value are you than the birds! And which of you by being anxious can add a single hour to his life? If then you are not able to do as a small as thing as that, why are you anxious about the rest? Consider the lilies, how they grow: they neither toil or spin, yet I tell you, even Solomon in all his glory was not arrayed like one of these. But if God so clothes the grass, which is alive in the field today, and tomorrow is

thrown in the oven, how much more will He clothe you. O you of little faith! And do not seek what you are to eat and what you are to drink, nor be worried. For all the nations of the world see after these things, and you r Father knows that you need them. Instead seek his kingdom and these things will be added to you. (Luke 12:22–31 ESV)

Wow. God will provide for us. Everything. Anything. Every day. We are cared for. No worries.

Seek God first, have faith, and live life free of anxiety. It is so hard to let go of worry and lean totally on God. It is a choice we have to make each day. I tell myself daily, "Let go and let God!" It is life changing. God is telling us not to worry about anything!

Listen to the Father. He knows all, and He will take care of us. "Do not merely listen to the word, and so deceive yourselves. Do what it says" (James 1:22 NIV) Go out in action each day doing what God said in His Word. Do not worry. Hakuna matata—no worries for the rest of our days!

Live in peace on this earth as much as you can. God will help you release your anxieties and fears until one day they are no more. Eternity in heaven will be perfect peace.

8   *Salvation*

THE DEFINITION OF SALVATION IS "BEING SAVED OR DELIVERED from some dire situation." Heaven is our salvation from this earth. Most may not think of this life on earth as a dire situation, but compared to the utter perfection and glorious joy of heaven, this earthly life is dire.

Of course, life has beauty and joy, but it also has pain and suffering. The gifts God gave us to enjoy on earth are not even close to the gifts that await us in heaven. I am grateful each day for salvation. It gives me hope, and it covers every aspect of my life. It is a blanket of hope for my saving day when I enter eternal salvation with my Father. I smile knowing that we will be totally free from earthly pain. "Truly my soul finds rest in God, my salvation comes from Him" (Psalm 62:1 NIV). I giggle with joy when I picture Seth's dream come true. He verbalizes his daily dream so clearly—his hope for heaven.

Seth has told me many things about salvation in innocent and beautiful words that hold so much truth, meaning, and hope. Seth said, "The day you go to heaven, you are never scared to leave your house because nothing about heaven is ever scary. You are just so happy you can't even handle it." Seth told me, "It's like this." He claps. "And you're in heaven. It's super speedy just like that." I am often amazed and astonished by Seth's statements; I cannot wrap my head around them. I asked, "That is so awesome, Seth. How do you know that?" "Jesus tells me," he said. Of course, Jesus speaks and Seth listens. Why would I ever wonder differently?

"We are confident, I say, and would prefer to be away from the body and at home with the Lord" (2 Corinthians 5:8 NIV). This verse is Seth's life song; he longs for heaven, he dreams of heaven, and he plans for heaven. Seth's love for Christ is so deep that he wants to be with Him again; he knows he belongs with Jesus. "Let your eyes look directly forward and your gaze be straight before you" (Proverbs 4:25 ESV). Seth's eyes are on heaven. If we could all grasp this and live this way God told us in His Word to live, our world would be a dramatically different place. "For our light and momentary troubles are achieving for us an eternal glory that far outweighs them all" (2 Corinthians 4:17 NIV).

God gave a gift to me through Seth, a gift I must share. Seth and God have changed my view of life. I look forward to heaven; our ultimate destination is known. I dwell on Jesus's perfect love. I plan for my reunion with the Lord. I knew none of this beforehand. None of it. I was overwhelmed and stressed, and I didn't see hope in my life, which seemed too tough for me. It wasn't as I had pictured it. It seemed so unfair. Every day, it was too hard.

Life is still complicated. I may not have an average day to day life but I have found peace within our struggles. I know you can as well. I could be overwhelmed and have no hope, but I am the opposite—I am joyful. I am beyond grateful. My heart sings with happiness and gratitude every day I get to wake up and serve my family and others.

God's incredible blessings swallow me whole every day. I am blessed that I can care for Seth every day. I am blessed my husband can work and supports us. I am blessed our needs are met each day. My blessings far outweigh the stress. I do not listen to the world any longer telling me what I should or shouldn't have in my life. I hear God telling me, "You are where you are for a reason. You have a purpose, so be steadfast and content. I will give you strength for each day. Conquer each day with joy. Your reward awaits you in heaven."

I smile, and my heart sings. I used to ponder my purpose until God spoke to me through his holy Word: "Truly I tell you, whatever you did for one of the least of these brothers and sisters of mine, you did for me" (Matthew 25:40 NIV).

My caregiving has a purpose. I would yearn to be back in action helping others and volunteering in church. I used to be so discontented; I felt my life had very little meaning. The mundane and ordinary that used to drive me crazy now propels me. I care for Seth's needs for the Lord's sake. It is important, so I do it with joy the best I can. Seth never feels like a burden; I offer my life and all I am to Christ. I pray each day to be molded into what God needs me to be. He is molding my heart into something beautiful.

Each day, I look forward to growing, changing, and finding more hope through God. I've found my purpose. Seth has shown me that we all share the same life purpose—to love and honor God and yearn for heaven. I look forward to the day when God will hold me in heaven and say, "Well done my good and faithful servant! You have been faithful with a few things, I will put you in charge of many things. Come and share you master's happiness" (Matthew 25:21 NIV). How my soul dances at this thought! How thankful I am for my life, for my journey. Seth and God have changed me. I am a constant work in progress. I have come so far but still have days where the darkness still creeps in. If you can relate, I encourage you to keep seeking and keep striving. God is shaping us each for His glory and His plan for us. Hold onto His light when life gets dark, lean into His love when you feel lonely. Press into His promises to fuel your faith. Keep looking up and looking forward. This world is not our home—heaven is. All that matters is heaven, Jesus, love and salvation.

Set your eyes on your future. Keep your head in the clouds. You were created for much more than this earth. Never lose sight of heaven's goodness. Relish God's earthly beauty. Watch the sunset; notice how the trees move in the wind. Glorify God with your every thought. Plan for heaven, and smile on thoughts of salvation. Watch your life be transformed. Say Seth's prayer: "Jesus, help me to be sweet like you." Feel God, seek God, adore God, and yearn for heaven to be with God.

Seth envisions the day he will have perfect peace, the day when he can run up and hug Jesus as hard as he can. When he can have no worries, outstretch his arms, and fly in unimaginable joy forever.

Thank you, Lord, that we have heaven awaiting us. Help us all to keep looking up to You and heaven and holding onto hope.

9 God's Plan

IN OUR FAMILY, WE ALWAYS SAY, "DON'T MAKE PLANS." WE actually never do. Seth's days are completely unpredictable, so we have learned the hard way that plans can and will change with little notice.

Everyone in our life knows that until we have made it to a destination, they shouldn't count on us being there. It's very hard to plan with Seth; each day is an unknown. I used to be so frustrated, but I have learned that our trials offer us the most valuable life lessons.

Only God knows our tomorrows, even our next five minutes; our future is all His. Knowing that God holds my future long and short term takes a whole lot of pressure off me. I trust Him; He knows all, He sees all, He created all, and He is all. I rest in His plan each day no matter the twists and turns that come.

He is steering us. "Trust in the Lord with all your heart and lean not on your own understanding; in all your ways submit to Him, and he will make your paths straight" (Proverbs 3:5 NIV). "Many are the plans in the mind of a man, but it is the purpose of the Lord that will stand" (Proverbs 19:21 NIV). My constant prayer is, "Your purpose over my plans Father. More of you and less of me."

Life can surprise us in beautiful and unexpected ways. I set this book down and began researching on how to get it published. I put down my pen, but God still had His in full motion. Only God knows the turns life would take for us; His plan all along was for this book to continue. So here I sit years later. Seth is ten. It's March 2018. Time flies. So much beauty, fear, and blessings have filled our life these past three years.

God has led us and continued to shape our lives in incredible ways that only He can. He answered my prayer of my heart's desire to reach others and share His love with them. The life of a stay-at-home mom and a full-time caregiver is lonely at times. I am inspired by a quote from Mother Teresa: "Don't worry about numbers. Help one person at a time and always start with the person nearest you." So I gave my whole heart to serving my family and reaching out to family and friends as much as I could. Then God spoke so clearly to me about learning a new craft. I have always loved art and loved to create.

When I was searching Etsy one night, God clearly said, "Learn how to make this." So with Him leading me, I set forward to learn a new craft. Now, I find so much joy and fulfillment with my Etsy page. It is a special place to me where I can share God's beauty and truth with others. It is my answered prayer. I am forever grateful for it and excited to see where God continues to lead me.

Seth has made miraculous gains in his life. He now attends his homeschool almost two hours a day and is learning to read. He is able to play outdoors more, and he enjoys spending time with his family and friends. Seth is sleeping in his own room and is so proud of how "big" he is. Things I didn't expect to change surely have. He has found his voice and no longer sits silently. He is a beautiful little chatterbox filled with sweet giggles and jokes. He has an adventurous side no one knew about, and he now flies with his daddy, which was one of his biggest fears! Go, Super Seth, go! God has truly worked countless miracles. We have more joy than ever. Our good days outweigh our bad days, and I am so grateful.

Never underestimate the amazing surprises God has in store. He is all knowing and all powerful. He is love.

Paintings I created with mustard seeds

10 The Solid Rock

I MENTIONED SETH'S ANXIETY BEFORE, BUT I WANT TO EXPLAIN how bad it was so you can appreciate the magnitude of the miracle God worked in our lives.

"Mommy, is our house strong?" "Will it ever get ruined?" Seth asked me such questions every day. At least thirty times a day, a circle of fear and anxiety surrounded him; he would obsess about our safety and sameness. Seth thrives on routine like most kids on the autism spectrum do. Seth had come far, but anxiety still remained.

On August 12, 2016, I woke up around five in the morning. There was a storm raging outside; the thunder and lightning scared me. I lay in bed praying for God to keep us and our home safe. I decided to go lie down with Seth so he wouldn't feel afraid. Not much later, my husband joined us.

The storm was fierce; we all felt a little frightened. I brought my prayers to God, and we decided to start our day early since we were all awake. I carried Seth to our master bathroom before we had breakfast, and I stepped in a puddle. I asked my husband to check for a roof leak, and we put towels down to soak up the puddle. We went into the living room and saw water coming in under every wall in our home. We were not leaking; we were flooding. Seth began screaming and crying. I panicked and started packing up essentials such as medication. My husband rushed outside to pull his truck up the road to a drier area so we wouldn't be stranded.

Water rushed in rapidly. Within ten minutes, we were ankle deep; everything was eerily floating. We had to leave. Seth kept asking if we would come back. I held back tears as he screamed for some beloved stuffed animals to take along. We grabbed all we could. My husband got our two dogs, and we escaped through our bedroom window into deeper floodwater.

We got in the truck. We were drenched, scared, and shoeless. I couldn't look back. We drove forward, and I prayed we would be safe. I was so afraid. Seth and I were physically ill with fear. Matt drove stoically, but I could tell he was shaken. His truck could barely make it out of our neighborhood. What should have been a fifteen-minute drive to my mother's home took three hours. Water everywhere. Stalled cars. It was a nightmare. I was terrified that we would be swept away by the floodwater and be separated.

Finally, by God's grace, we crossed a water-covered bridge safely and made it to a dry road. We were safe. God had answered my plea, my cry, my prayer. I felt so much relief. I looked at my sweet Seth. I felt ill again. I wondered how he would cope with this, what kind of regression this would cause. We had come so far, but this was too much. His biggest fear, all so scary. I prayed. I couldn't bring home back. I couldn't erase this frightful memory in our lives. I knew that our normal would never be the same again. I braced for the impact this would have.

Then a calm came within our storm, a calm I hadn't seen coming. I know that God can and will move mountains, that He is on our side, but so often, I underestimate His power. Seth not only handled this twist on our path; he also walked through it with joy! We stayed with my gracious aunt and uncle for three nights, and Seth did wonderfully.

They watched Seth for us when we could finally return home to see what it looked like. I felt ill driving home. I didn't want to see our home we had lived and loved in for over a decade in ruins, but

God gave me strength. I walked in to find my photos were okay. I was overjoyed that I got to keep my precious memories.

Our home, however, smelled nauseating. The mess was dreadful and overwhelming. We had friends and family help us clear our home and start the demo process. Seeing everything we worked for on the curb was heart-wrenching; it was all trash. But it was just stuff, I reminded myself. I chose to focus on the fact that my family was safe. We were okay, and this would be okay too. Everything could be replaced. However, to Seth, our things were his joy, comfort and reliable source of calm. Our home was his safe place in this unpredictable world. This was especially true with his stuffed animals, whom he referred to as his friends.

Nothing could have prepared us for the physical exhaustion we felt that day. It remained hard and constant, but we found a bit of rest after moving into our rental house. It was nonetheless unfamiliar, and we all felt pretty lost. We didn't have much and what we did have had been tossed about haphazardly. It was overwhelming. But when I looked at Seth, my heart found some relief. He was handling the storm around us with remarkable joy. He was more than okay. That was a miracle that took my breath away. God blessed Seth and us with peace and joy at a time when peace and joy should have been hard to come by. God showed us daily that we were safe and that was all that mattered. This house wasn't home, but we were together, and that fact trumped everything we were facing. Home truly is where the heart is.

Seth decided he wanted to make cookies for other families who had been flooded out in our community. Through the process of baking and sharing joy with others, we came to learn one of our favorite life lessons thus far—never let your trials harden your heart. When you are walking through a difficult time or season, step away from your burden and be a blessing to others. It is the quickest and most beautiful way to lift your spirits and renew your heart.

After months of hard work, God answered our prayers again; we were able to move home for Christmas and celebrate Christ's birth in our home. Our hearts were overjoyed. Though we were surrounded by boxes and construction to be done, I look back on that Christmas as one of our sweetest. "To him who is able to do immeasurably more than we all ask or imagine, according to His power that is at work within us" (Ephesians 3:20 NIV).

God is more than capable of moving the mountains in your life. He will work in ways that will leave you no doubt that His power is intricately woven into each detail of your life.

That flood, that trial has shown us that God is our solid rock; we cannot and will not be shaken.

> Anyone who listens to my teaching and follows it is wise, like a person who builds a house on solid rock. Though the rain comes in torrents and the floodwaters rise and the winds beat up against that house, it won't collapse because it is built on solid rock. But anyone who hears my teaching and doesn't obey it is foolish, like a person who builds a house on sand. When the rains and floods come and the winds beat against that house it will collapse with a mighty crash. (Matthew 7:24–27 NLT)

God is by our side. He is strong. He is mighty. We will not fall or perish because God is our solid rock.

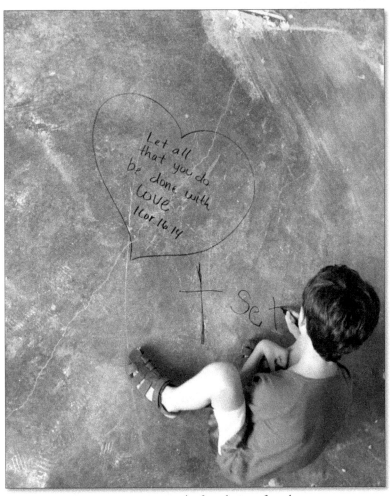

Writing scripture on the foundation of our home
while renovating after the flood

Seth's cookies for other families that had been flooded out

11 Mustard Seeds and Music

TYPICALLY, MUSTARD SEEDS AND MUSIC DO NOT GO together, but in our lives, they stand tall as a pillar of God's goodness in our lives. Matthew 17:20 (ESV) tells us, "Truly I tell you, if you have faith as small as a mustard seed, you can say to this mountain, 'move from here to hear,' and it will move. Nothing will be impossible for you."

When God spoke to me about using crafts and art to share His love with others, a tiny mustard seed became the springboard for so much goodness. When we take even a small step forward in our faith, God smiles with joy. When we step forward in trust, God will leads us, carry us, and give us more than we need to succeed. He helps us climb mountains in our lives and do the unthinkable; He shows us that with Him, all things are possible.

Our hardships are vital for us to grow and change. God has a purpose for us, and He will work things out for good. Romans 8:28 (NIV) tells us, "And we know that all things work together for good to them who love God, to them who are called according to His purpose."

I see clearly now how God has worked to mold and shape me. Each time of darkness was an opportunity to see His light. His love is breathtaking; He never gives up on us, and he holds us as we grow. Through His gift to me of Seth and every struggle along the way, I no longer feel my life is useless. I no longer feel empty even though much of my circumstances remain the same. The mundane routine of my life is my beautiful. Instead of lying in a pit of self-pity, I look up to God. I look around at His beauty and blessings. I know that in every difficult moment, God is working on me. I ask myself, *What can I learn from this?* I pray for strength and obedience. I excitedly move forward each day. I know that God has a purpose and that He is good. I have faith that God will move mountains for you as well.

"Speaking to one another with Psalms, hymns and songs from the Spirit. Sing and make music from your heart to the Lord" (Ephesians 5:19 NIV). Life is more inspiring and less lonely when you have music, right? Music is medicine. It can uplift, encourage, comfort, and energize you.

Until this year, our life was silent in terms of music. Any background noise was like nails on a chalkboard to Seth. Music overloaded his already overloaded brain until one day that we listened to a song and he tolerated it. He actually enjoyed it. So we listened to and learned each word to that song, and it was magical! A welcomed gift in our usual silence at home or riding in the car. "I will sing of your love and justice to you Lord, I will sing praise" (Psalm 101:1 NIV).

We often don't realize how valuable something is until it is no longer consistent, until it is gone. Once music came back into our lives, it brought pure and abundant joy. I can't put into words the joy my hear feels when I peek into my rearview mirror and see Seth singing, smiling, and enjoying music. His love for music has blossomed, and we now have a playlist of our favorite Christian songs.

Our music time is our worship time. We sing in praise, worship, joy, and thanksgiving to God. God's Word through music inspires and shapes our hearts. We become more filled with Him and focused on Him. Oh, the joy of singing to God with my boy! Psalm

98:4–6 (NIV) tells us, "Shout for joy to the Lord, all the earth, burst into jubilant song with music; make music to the Lord with the harp and the sound of singing with trumpets and the blast of the ram's horn-shout for joy before the Lord, the King."

There is my word. I feel jubilant when I get to sing with my son! Feeling or expressing great happiness and triumph is the definition of jubilance. May we all live jubilantly for God music or not. God alone is all we need to be utterly and completely overwhelmed with joy. Singing to Him in worship is a wonderful and lovely way to allow our hearts to praise Him and be filled with Him.

I am so grateful for the wonderful surprises of mustard seeds and music God has planted in our lives. I know that God's timing is perfect and that His purpose is greater than our plans.

Never question if God is working because His almighty fingerprints are on everything in our journeys. Don't stop going forward. Keep trusting and watching God's perfect purpose unfold before you. "Let the message of Christ dwell among you richly as you teach and admonish one another with all wisdom through psalms, hymns, and songs from the Spirit, singing to God with gratitude in your hearts" (Colossians 3:16 NIV).

Seth and I embracing the beauty of the sunset

A creation of mine and my answered prayer of
sharing God's love with others

12 The Giants

A CHAMPION IS SOMEONE WHO HAS DEFEATED OR SURPASSED all rivals in a competition. A champion is a winner. In 1 Samuel 17:4, Goliath was described as a champion, a huge, towering, strong, and well-armed champion. This giant, however, met his match when God called David to defeat him with a single stone. This Bible account is a must read; it is an inspiration. On our fridge hangs a coloring book picture colored by Seth of David and his stone preparing for battle. We see it each day and draw strength from this scripture.

I will dig deeper into this scripture and how it applies to us all. It has brought so much courage to Seth knowing that if God calls us to do something no matter how impossible or scary it may seem, God will equip us to succeed.

What giants are lurking in our lives? What are the scariest and most intimidating things in our lives today that we find hard to stand up to? We all have giants, and some are more frightful than others. God uses the giants in our lives for His glory just as He did with David. When can step up in confidence and face the things we fear the most, that is God. God gives us strength to do what we cannot. When the impossible takes place, God is working. To God be the glory.

God has equipped us to conquer the giants in our lives countless times. One of my most recent giants was the possibility of our being flooded again. I struggle with debilitating fear any time I hear rain. Every emotion I felt the morning we flooded comes back to me. It is hard for me to deal with that fear especially when my husband is out of town. The fear grips me and doesn't let go. I spend many nights praying and listening.

One night as I heard rain coming down, my heart was beating faster and faster, but I heard God say, "Just trust me. The future is in my hands, and it is not yours to fear. I will take care of you no matter what. I always do." Instead of feeling full relief, I came back with, "I know, God, but this fear takes over not just my mind but my body as well." God spoke so clearly again telling me that if I would let my fear go, He would take care of that as well. Over time and after lots of prayer, fear loosened its grip on me.

God loves us more than we know. He is standing ready to help us, to carry us. Often, we stand in the way and hold onto fear, worry, and concerns. We must let them go so God can steady our hearts, calm our minds, and lead us to courage each day. God reminds me often and through Seth of what a childlike faith is. "Truly I tell you anyone who will not receive the kingdom of God like a little child will never enter it" (Mark 10:15 NIV).

We are God's treasured children. Any parent wants what is best for his or her children and doesn't want to see them living in fear. Children are comforted by the presence of their parents; they feel safe and secure. They go in the direction their parents lead because they trust that they know best.

May we hold our Father's hands tightly, trust Him fully, never doubt He knows what is best, and never second-guess His purpose. We should walk with Him in trust and childlike dependence because He is God. He knows all and will care for us in ways we couldn't imagine if only we can let go and let Him. "Be still and know that I am God" (Psalm 46:10 NIV).

"For the Lord sees not as man sees: man looks on the outward appearance, but The Lord looks on the heart" (1 Samuel 16:7 NKJV). A giant in my life I thought I would never conquer was low self-esteem. It didn't fit into my book as a part of longing for heaven, but it affected my ability to enjoy the life God gave me while waiting to return home to heaven.

For my entire life, I never felt good enough physically or emotionally. Maybe you can relate. The pressure to look a certain way was beyond my comprehension, and it has always consumed me. The pressure to fit in has also been heavy on my heart. I never felt beautiful in my life until God worked miracles in my heart. I didn't like my reflection and always thought I didn't have enough gifts, talents, or education to contribute. I began to rid my life of negativity in entertainment, in reading, and in social media. I replaced all I watched and read with Christian people who were warriors to me, who spoke God's truth boldly.

I read book after book digging deeper into scripture. God's Word reshaped my view on life. I began to focus on my heart, on wanting to be more like Christ instead of more like the world. I would see a flaw and count it as a blessing because God doesn't make mistakes. I often tell Seth the same, that God made him perfect in every way. "For You created my inmost being; You knit me together in my mother's womb" (Psalm 139:13 NIV).

We are the work of God's mighty hands exactly as He intended. That is a beautiful thing. Look into your heart, not your reflection in the mirror. See if your heart is reflecting God's grace. Allow your heart to shine so others can see His love, peace, and joy. Your heart is what matters.

Once my confidence was emerging and I no longer obsessed over the way I looked, my life took a wonderful turn. I was able to find my purpose and live it out with boldness. Others may think I need to live different from the way I do, but God is the only opinion that matters. I live to please Him; I live for Him, and I want my life to be a love song for Him alone. I finally am at peace with my gifts, talents, and attributes. God uncovered all the beauty hiding in my aching heart. He uncovered the strength we all hold to let go of insecurities and stand firm in Him. A giant I never thought I would see fall after thirty-two years of life did fall, and I still beam with joy that God equipped me to conquer it. "For God has not given us a spirit of fear, but of power, and of love and of a sound mind" (2 Timothy 1:7 NKJV).

He created each of us with unique gifts and a wonderful purpose for Him. "For we are His workmanship, created in Christ Jesus for good works, which God prepared beforehand, that we should walk in them" (Ephesians 2:10 ESV).

Hold onto His truth because you—all of us—are beautiful. We all have a purpose. I try my hardest to instill this in Seth as well. He knows he is different and behind his peers in many ways, but he also knows that God doesn't make mistakes and that He has Seth exactly where He needs him to be.

Seth has defeated giant after giant in his short life by the grace of God. He is such a different child today than he was just a couple of years ago. People who see him now can't believe the wonderful strides he has made. His silence has been replaced with sweet chatter and jokes. His anxiety in social settings has turned to joyful smiles and interaction. The appointments and medical tests that had caused him to throw violent fits for hours no longer upset this calm and brave young boy. His anxieties had been so severe that even Valium couldn't contain them, but now, his fear is gone.

He is going to school each day and sleeping alone as well. Huge victories. The giants have been defeated with and by God's power. All miracles, all God! God is equipping Seth to face down the Goliaths in his life in a way that makes others take note. His full and perfect power is on display. Seth will tell you, "I was scared, and I'm just not anymore." To see Seth conquering difficulties in life makes me feel weightless with relief, jubilant in joy, and in awe of God's love. "The Lord gives strength to His people; the Lord blesses His people with peace" (Psalm 29:11 NIV).

Strength and peace are vital parts of a joyful and fulfilled life, but they are out of our grasp without God. God loves us more than we can comprehend, and He will allow us to be champions of our lives, to be winners, to succeed. "Neither height nor depth, nor anything else in all creation; will be able to separate us from the love of God that is in Christ Jesus our Lord" (Romans 8:39 NIV). He will never leave us. He will always love us, and we will not be defeated.

Seth once told me as he was staring at his shadow, "Your shadow reminds you that God is always on your side, always right next to you." "Be strong and courageous, do not be afraid. For the Lord your God will be with you wherever you go" (Joshua 1:9 NIV).

Let's keep looking up. Let's hold onto our Father's hand, trust His lead, and walk in peace and joy until our greatest hopes for our future become reality when we are finally home, home at last in heaven!

Seth telling me his shadow is a reminder that God is always at your side

13 Change Is a Good Thing?

L IFE IS CONSTANTLY CHANGING. ONE THING IS CERTAIN— change. Seasons change, people change, and life changes. Change can be a remarkable blessing in life, a turnaround you didn't expect, an answered prayer.

Change can also be devastating—the loss of a loved one, an illness, or an injury no one saw coming. I find insurmountable comfort in the truth that Christ is unchanging. He is eternally unchanging and will never leave our side. "Jesus is the same yesterday, today and forever" (Hebrews 13:8 NIV). "The Lord is with me; I will not be afraid" (Psalm 118:6 NIV).

I have watched Seth change in his faith. His head is not in the clouds as much as it once was. As he makes strides on earth, he is less concentrated on heaven, but he is consistent in sharing God with everyone. His heart is so sweet, kind, and giving. I watched my son kiss his great-grandmother goodbye with more bravery than an adult would have. He stepped out of the room and told our family that she was going to love heaven. He reassured us of the joy, beauty, and pain-free eternity she was headed for.

He continues to share and nourish others' faith and trust in God. As he grows, his faith is sometimes questioned. When he comes to me with questions or has days when he feels hopeless, I thank God. The journey we have been on in these past ten years has completely overhauled my heart. My faith continues to grow but has come so far because of God speaking through my son. With this transformation of my heart, I can now stand with God's help and guide my son through his walk in faith.

My child showed me to have a childlike dependence on God alone, and I will show him the same. Seeing this shift in our life enlightened my soul to an often-asked question of why. Why does God allow difficult seasons in our lives? Why does God allow pain, heartache, and tragedy? We will never have all these answers, but we aren't supposed to.

I think that sometimes, we are called to walk through trials so we can learn from it and have compassion for others walking through the same. We can be their comfort and light as they journey the road we once did or maybe still are. Just as Jesus humbled Himself in the ultimate sacrifice and became human, He knows the struggles we face on earth. He helps us and guides us, and He is full of compassion. "Two are better than one ... If either of them falls down, one can help the other up" (Ecclesiastes 4:9–10 NIV). I know that without the trials in my life, I would not have been transformed. I stand ready to learn and grow more each day, to reach out and help others as they face their difficulties on earth as well. I share with them the wisdom Seth shared with me that the hope of heaven is real and that everything will turn out more than okay.

God is unchanging; He will always be in control. He sees our first breath and our last. He knows the number of hairs on our heads. His love is deeper than our minds can fathom. Change in our life will come, and fear will settle in, but that is part of life. This earth isn't perfect, but heaven is. We can rest in God's truth. We can look up to Him and His peace and love. With God, change can be a good thing even when it's bad.

God says He will work all for good for those who love Him. His truth in the Bible also reveals He withholds no good thing from us. "For The Lord God is a sun and shield: The Lord will give grace and glory: no good thing will He withhold from them that walk uprightly" (Psalm 84:11 KJV). When life is filled with change, it can be scary, and this scripture might not make much sense. If no good things are withheld from us, why is it so hard?

We think good equals pleasant or easy, but good by definition is to be desired or approved of. I don't think any of us would desire or approve of a difficult or tragic change in our lives, but God never withholds His good things—His presence, strength, hope, and everlasting and perfect love. All of His things are amazingly great! I pray we can all yield to the One who knows all and is all. God's purpose will always be greater than our plans.

Let us trust Him as we journey through life. Let us press into all the good things He has for us here and now and for His good purposes yet to be fulfilled. May we take our daily bread one step at a time hand in hand with Him. May we never fail to look up and look around at His majestic beauty and blessings surrounding us.

I pray that when our future crosses our minds, we will think of heaven first. Our destination is known; it is a promise, a guarantee. I pray that we can live with our minds set on things above. I pray that we know our time on earth is fleeting and that we try to live every day to its fullest without worry or fear weighing us down. We have faith, we have hope, we have love, and we have strength all from God as we keep moving forward and looking up. We have heaven ahead of us, and that is a beautiful thing.

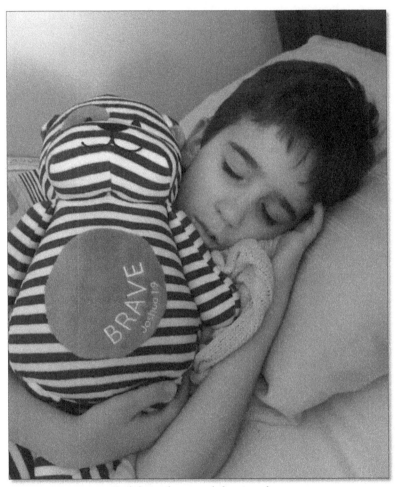

Seth being brave and sleeping alone

Seth flying with his dad, a huge fear he once had has vanished

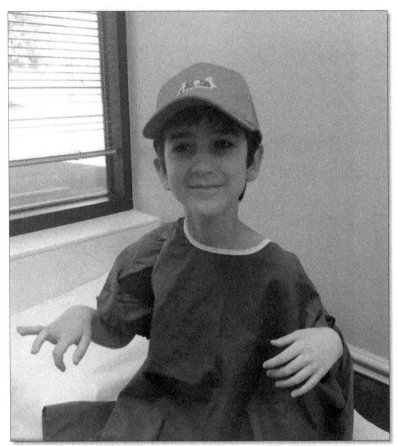

Fearless at his doctor's appointment

A cross at sunset; God's beauty is a constant

About the Author

WITH A DEEP LONGING TO SHARE HER STORY OF RENEWING faith and unshakable joy, Emily Wolf began to write. Emily is a wife and mother with an ambitious heart for Jesus. She has seen God move mountains in her life.

Her only child, her son, Seth inspired this book. She felt deeply that his relationship with Jesus was powerful and needed to be shared. His excitement for heaven from a very young age was nothing short of incredible. Through Seth's faith, Emily's eyes and heart were opened to so much she had never known, so much she maybe would have never discovered.

Destination Known is her story, her family's walk with Christ. This book is laced with scripture to inspire you just as she has been. The message throughout this book is one of God's unwavering presence and eternal love. It is filled with hope that no matter what you are facing, God is with us each step of the way, that no matter the pain, God always has a purpose, that no matter the path, it will lead to your ultimate destination, your home—heaven.

CPSIA information can be obtained
at www.ICGtesting.com
Printed in the USA
LVHW040017050319
609518LV00001B/19/P